G000155871

everyday
cocktails

Bath New York Singapore Hong Kong Cologne Delhi Melbourne

This edition published by Parragon in 2009

Parragon
Queen Street House
4 Queen Street
Bath BA1 1HE, UK

ISBN: 978-1-4075-5623-9
Printed in China

Cover by Talking Design
Designed by Terry Jeavons & Company

Notes for the Reader
This book uses both metric and imperial measurements. Follow the same units of measurement throughout; do not mix metric and imperial. All spoon measurements are level: teaspoons are assumed to be 5 ml, and tablespoons are assumed to be 15 ml. Unless otherwise stated, milk is assumed to be full fat, eggs and individual vegetables are medium, and pepper is freshly ground black pepper.

The times given are an approximate guide only. Preparation times differ according to the techniques used by different people and the cooking times may also vary from those given. Optional ingredients, variations or serving suggestions have not been included in the calculations.

Recipes using raw or very lightly cooked eggs should be avoided by infants, the elderly, pregnant women, convalescents and anyone suffering from an illness. Pregnant and breastfeeding women are advised to avoid eating peanuts and peanut products. Sufferers from nut allergies should be aware that some of the ready-made ingredients used in the recipes in this book may contain nuts. Always check the packaging before use.

everyday
cocktails

introduction

From the classic sophistication of a dry martini to the juicy delights of a fruit daiquiri and from the elegance of a julep to a colourful shooter, cocktails are as much a delight to the eyes as to the palate. They are flavoursome, fun and designed to be shared – but as they are often potent, moderation is a useful word to keep in mind.

They are simply mixed drinks, usually based on one or more spirits or liqueurs and flavoured with fruit juices, syrups, spices and other mixers. (Non-alcoholic cocktails are generally based on fruit or vegetable juices.) The flavours blend harmoniously, the drinks look appealing and although they have a 'kick', they won't go

straight to your head. Clearly, there is more to making a cocktail than simply tipping the contents of half a dozen bottles into a shaker. Fortunately, hundreds of cocktails have been created and tested regularly since the first great cocktail era of the 1920s and new recipes are being devised all the time.

Cocktails may be shaken or stirred – the former are cloudy because they contain egg white, cream or fruit juices, while the latter  are clear. A cocktail shaker is not essential but makes mixing easier and you feel more professional. Pour the ingredients into the shaker over cracked ice, fit the lids, shake vigorously until the outside of the shaker is lightly frosted, then pour through a strainer (usually incorporated in the shaker) into glasses. However, make sure that you never add fizzy mixers, such as tonic water, to the shaker. If they form part of the cocktail, top up with them once the drink has been poured. You can also use a blender and this is sometimes specified

in the recipes for certain cocktails. Stirred cocktails are made by pouring the ingredients over cracked ice into a mixing glass – basically a translucent glass jug – and stirred with a long-handled spoon before being strained into appropriate serving glasses. You can also use the goblet part of a cocktail shaker.

vodka & gin

Vodka, distilled from grain and filtered through charcoal, has long been a popular base for cocktails because it is a neutral spirit and virtually flavourless. This means that it mixes well with any number of liqueurs and non-alcoholic mixers, adding weight to the cocktail without affecting the flavour. Consequently, there are not only numerous classics based on vodka, but it is also often the spirit of choice for contemporary concoctions.

Recently, flavoured vodkas – lemon, pepper, peach, cinnamon, chocolate, chilli and many others – have become fashionable. Although these are most often served straight, they have introduced a new dimension to cocktails. Adventurous would-be bartenders might like to try substituting one of these for standard vodka. Choose one that complements the main flavour of the drink.

Gin is also distilled from grain but it is then infused with 'botanicals', including juniper which gives it both its name and characteristic flavour. It is the base of many famous cocktails, the most celebrated of which must be the Martini. It is a popular choice for the classic cocktail served in a small V-shaped glass because it works well with other spirits, liqueurs and alcoholic drinks, but it is also frequently used as the base for longer, thirst-quenching coolers.

cosmopolitan

ingredients

SERVES 1

2 measures vodka

1 measure triple sec

1 measure fresh lime juice

1 measure cranberry juice

ice

orange peel twist, to decorate

method

1 Shake the first four ingredients over the ice until well frosted.

2 Strain into a chilled cocktail glass.

3 Dress with the twist of orange peel.

metropolitan

ingredients

SERVES 1

1 lemon wedge

1 tbsp caster sugar

cracked ice

$1/2$ measure vodka

$1/2$ measure framboise

$1/2$ measure cranberry juice

$1/2$ measure orange juice

method

1 Rub the rim of a cocktail glass with the lemon wedge and dip into the sugar.

2 Put the ice into a shaker and pour in the liquid ingredients.

3 Cover and shake for 10–20 seconds, until the outside of the shaker is misted.

4 Strain into the glass.

vodkatini

ingredients

SERVES 1

1 measure vodka
ice
dash dry vermouth
lime peel twist, to decorate

method

1 Pour the vodka over a handful of the ice in a mixing glass.

2 Add the vermouth, stir well, and strain into a cocktail glass.

3 Dress with the twist of lime peel.

the legend martini

ingredients

SERVES 1

2 measures iced vodka

1 measure blackberry liqueur

1 measure fresh lime juice

dash sugar syrup

method

1 Shake all the ingredients together until really well frosted.

2 Strain into a chilled martini glass.

the modern martini

ingredients

SERVES 1

1 very ripe pomegranate
2 measures vodka
ice

method

1 Spoon the flesh of the pomegranate into a shaker and lightly crush.

2 Add the vodka and ice and shake well.

3 Strain into a chilled martini glass.

bloody mary

ingredients

SERVES 1

dash Worcestershire sauce

dash Tabasco sauce

cracked ice

2 measures vodka

splash dry sherry

6 measures tomato juice

juice $1/2$ lemon

pinch celery salt

pinch cayenne pepper

celery stick with leaves and lemon slice, to decorate

method

1 Pour the Worcestershire sauce and Tabasco sauce over the ice in a shaker and add the vodka, sherry, tomato juice and lemon juice.

2 Shake vigorously until frosted.

3 Strain into a tall chilled glass, add a pinch of celery salt and a pinch of cayenne pepper and decorate with the celery stick and the slice of lemon.

long island iced tea

ingredients

SERVES 1

2 measures vodka

1 measure gin

1 measure white tequila

1 measure white rum

$1/2$ measure white crème de menthe

2 measures lemon juice

1 tsp sugar syrup

cracked ice

cola

lime wedge, to decorate

method

1 Shake the first seven ingredients vigorously over the ice until well frosted.

2 Strain into an ice-filled tall glass and top up with the cola.

3 Dress with the lime wedge.

sex on the beach

ingredients

SERVES 1

1 measure peach schnapps

1 measure vodka

2 measures fresh orange juice

3 measures cranberry and peach juice

ice

dash lemon juice

orange peel, to decorate

method

1 Shake the first four ingredients over the ice until well frosted.

2 Strain into an ice-filled glass and squeeze on the lemon juice.

3 Dress with the orange peel.

moscow mule

ingredients

SERVES 1

2 measures vodka

1 measure lime juice

cracked ice

ginger beer

lime slice, to decorate

method

1 Shake the vodka and lime juice vigorously over the ice until well frosted.

2 Half fill a chilled tall glass with cracked ice and strain the cocktail over it.

3 Top up with ginger beer and dress with the slice of lime.

screwdriver

ingredients

SERVES 1

cracked ice
2 measures vodka
orange juice
orange slice, to decorate

method

1 Fill a chilled glass with the cracked ice. Pour the vodka over the ice and top up with orange juice.

2 Stir well to mix and dress with the slice of orange.

black russian

ingredients

SERVES 1

2 measures vodka
1 measure coffee liqueur
cracked ice
ice cubes

method

1 Pour the vodka and coffee liqueur over the cracked ice in a small chilled glass.

2 Add the ice cubes and stir to mix.

kamikaze

ingredients

SERVES 1

1 measure vodka

1 measure triple sec

$^1/_2$ measure fresh lime juice

$^1/_2$ measure fresh lemon juice

ice

dry white wine, chilled

slices of cucumber and lime, to decorate

method

1 Shake the vodka, triple sec, lime juice and lemon juice together over the ice until well frosted.

2 Strain into a chilled glass and top up with wine.

3 Dress with the slices of cucumber and lime.

harvey wallbanger

ingredients

SERVES 1

ice

3 measures vodka

8 measures orange juice

2 tsp Galliano

cherry and orange slice, to decorate

method

1 Half fill a tall glass with the ice, pour the vodka and orange juice over and float Galliano on top.

2 Dress with the cherry and the slice of orange.

singapore sling

ingredients

SERVES 1

2 measures gin
1 measure cherry brandy
1 measure lemon juice
1 tsp grenadine
cracked ice
soda water
lime peel and cocktail cherries, to decorate

method

1 Shake the gin, cherry brandy, lemon juice and grenadine vigorously over the ice until well frosted.

2 Half fill a chilled glass with cracked ice and strain in the cocktail.

3 Top up with soda water and dress with the lime peel and cocktail cherries.

slow comfortable screw

ingredients

SERVES 1

2 measures sloe gin

orange juice

cracked ice

orange slice, to decorate

method

1 Shake the sloe gin and orange juice over the ice until well frosted and pour into a chilled glass.

2 Dress with the slice of orange.

martini

ingredients

SERVES 1

3 measures gin

1 tsp dry vermouth, or to taste

cracked ice

green cocktail olive, to decorate

method

1 Pour the gin and vermouth over the ice in a mixing glass and stir well to mix.

2 Strain into a chilled cocktail glass and dress with the cocktail olive.

oasis

ingredients

SERVES 1

1 measure blue curaçao

2 measures gin

soda water

ice

ice cubes

lemon wedges, to decorate

method

1 Shake the first two ingredients over the ice until well frosted.

2 Strain into a chilled cocktail glass and top up with the soda water.

3 Add the ice cubes and dress with the wedges of lemon.

moonlight

ingredients

SERVES 4

3 measures grapefruit juice

4 measures gin

1 measure kirsch

4 measures white wine

$^1/_2$ tsp lemon zest

ice

method

1 Shake all the ingredients together well and strain into chilled glasses.

mississippi mule

ingredients

SERVES 1

2 measures gin
$^1/_2$ measure cassis
$^1/_2$ measure lemon juice
crushed ice

method

1 Shake the liquid ingredients vigorously over the ice until well frosted.

2 Strain over crushed ice into a small chilled tumbler.

dry martini

ingredients

SERVES 1

1 measure London Dry Gin

dash dry vermouth

ice

olive, to decorate

method

1 Shake the gin and vermouth over the ice until well frosted and combined.

2 Strain into a chilled glass.

3 Dress with the olive.

road runner

ingredients

SERVES 1

2 measures gin
$1/2$ measure dry vermouth
$1/2$ measure Pernod
1 tsp grenadine
cracked ice

method

1 Shake the gin, vermouth, Pernod and grenadine vigorously over the ice until well frosted.

2 Strain into a chilled glass.

tom collins

ingredients

SERVES 1

3 measures gin
2 measures lemon juice
$^1/_2$ measure sugar syrup
cracked ice
soda water
lemon slice, to decorate

method

1 Shake the gin, lemon juice and sugar syrup vigorously over the ice until well frosted.

2 Strain into a chilled tumbler and top up with soda water.

3 Dress with the slice of lemon.

white lady

ingredients

SERVES 1

2 measures gin
1 measure triple sec
1 measure lemon juice
cracked ice

method

1 Shake the gin, triple sec and lemon juice vigorously over the ice until well frosted.

2 Strain into a chilled cocktail glass.

my fair lady

ingredients

SERVES 1

1 measure gin

$^1/_2$ measure lemon juice

$^1/_2$ measure orange juice

$^1/_2$ measure fraise

1 egg white

ice

method

1 Shake the first five ingredients over ice and strain into a cocktail glass.

tequila & rum

Distilled from the fermented, steam-cooked heart of the cactus-like *Agave tequilana*, the Mexican spirit tequila is a relative newcomer to the cocktail menu. It may have been a late starter but it has certainly made up for lost time and tequila-based cocktails are now among the most popular. The pale-coloured Margarita, served in a salt-rimmed glass with a slice of lime, is an instantly recognizable cocktail icon. There are two types of tequila. Silver tequila is matured only briefly, usually in stainless steel vats. It is colourless and a little rough on the throat. Golden tequila is matured for at least three years in oak vats. It is golden in colour, mellow in flavour and more expensive.

Rum, distilled from the fermented sap of sugar cane, comes in three distinctive types, making it a very versatile spirit as a base for cocktails. Light-bodied white rum, which is actually colourless and clear, is widely used in classic-style cocktails. It is aged for just one year. Golden rum is made in the same way as white rum but is matured for three years, resulting in a more mellow flavour and a golden colour. Dark rum has a much more powerful flavour because it is matured for five or more years in wooden barrels. It is then blended and may be darkened with caramel. It is the best choice for punches.

margarita

ingredients

SERVES 1

lime wedge, plus an extra wedge to decorate

coarse salt

cracked ice

3 measures white tequila

1 measure triple sec

2 measures lime juice

method

1 Rub the rim of a chilled cocktail glass with the lime wedge and then dip in salt to frost.

2 Put the ice into a cocktail shaker. Pour over the liquid ingredients. Shake vigorously until a frost forms.

3 Strain into the prepared glass and dress with the lime wedge.

margarita shot

ingredients

SERVES 8

$^1/_2$ lime, cut into wedges

2 tbsp fine salt

1 packet lime jelly

1 cup hot water

4 tbsp Cointreau

225 ml/8 fl oz tequila

method

1 Rub the rims of eight shot glasses with lime, then dip in salt.

2 Place the jelly in a large heatproof measuring jug. Add the hot water and stir until the jelly has dissolved. Leave to cool, then stir in the Cointreau and tequila to make up to 450 ml/16 fl oz.

3 Divide between the prepared glasses and chill until set.

tequila cocktail

ingredients

SERVES 1

cracked ice

2 measures tequila

1 tbsp cranberry juice

method

1 Put the ice into a cocktail shaker with the tequila and cranberry juice.

2 Shake vigorously until well frosted, then strain into a chilled cocktail glass.

tequila mockingbird

ingredients

SERVES 1

2 measures white tequila

1 measure white crème de menthe

1 measure fresh lime juice

cracked ice

method

1 Shake the tequila, crème de menthe and lime juice vigorously over the ice until well frosted.

2 Strain into a chilled highball glass.

tequila sunrise

ingredients

SERVES 1

2 parts silver tequila
cracked ice
orange juice
1 measure grenadine

method

1 Pour the tequila over the ice in a chilled highball glass and top up with orange juice. Stir well to mix.

2 Slowly pour in the grenadine.

tequila slammer

ingredients

SERVES 1

1 measure chilled white tequila

1 measure lemon juice

chilled sparkling wine

method

1 Put the tequila and lemon juice into a chilled glass. Top up with sparkling wine.

2 Cover the glass with your hand and slam.

jack frost

ingredients
SERVES 1

3/4 measure blue curaçao, iced

icing sugar

1 measure chilled tequila

2 measures chilled cream

crushed ice

method

1 Dip the rim of a medium-sized cocktail glass in the curaçao, shake off any excess and dip immediately in sugar. Set aside in a cold place to dry and set.

2 Shake the rest of the curaca, tequila and the cream over the ice until well frosted.

3 Pour carefully into the glass.

mad dog

ingredients

SERVES 1

1 measure white tequila

1 measure crème de banane

1 measure white crème de cacao

1/2 measure lime juice

cracked ice

lime and banana slices and a cocktail cherry, to decorate

method

1 Shake the first four ingredients vigorously over the ice until well frosted.

2 Strain into a chilled cocktail glass and dress with the fruit.

shady lady

ingredients

SERVES 1

3 measures tequila

1 measure apple brandy

1 measure cranberry juice

dash lime juice

ice

method

1 Shake the ingredients over the ice until well frosted.

2 Strain into a chilled cocktail glass.

wild night out

ingredients

SERVES 1

3 measures white tequila

2 measures cranberry juice

1 measure lime juice

cracked ice

ice cubes

soda water

method

1 Shake the first three ingredients vigorously over the ice until well frosted.

2 Half fill a chilled glass with the ice cubes and strain the cocktail over them. Add soda water to taste.

piña colada

ingredients

SERVES 1

crushed ice

2 measures white rum

1 measure dark rum

3 measures pineapple juice

2 measures coconut cream

pineapple wedges, to decorate

method

1 Mix some crushed ice in a blender with the white rum, dark rum, pineapple juice and coconut cream until smooth.

2 Pour, without straining, into a tall, chilled glass and dress with the pineapple wedges.

casablanca

ingredients

SERVES 1

3 measures white rum

4 measures pineapple juice

2 measures coconut cream

crushed ice

pineapple wedge, to decorate

method

1 Shake the first three ingredients together over the ice and strain into a cocktail glass.

2 Dress with the pineapple wedge.

black widow

ingredients

SERVES 1

2/3 measure dark rum

1/3 measure Southern Comfort

juice 1/2 lime

dash curaçao

ice

soda water

lime peel twist, to decorate

method

1 Shake the first four ingredients well together over the ice and strain into a chilled tumbler.

2 Top up with soda water to taste and dress with the twist of lime peel.

mellow mule

ingredients

SERVES 1

2 measures white rum

1 measure dark rum

1 measure golden rum

1 measure Falernum (wine-based ginger syrup)

1 measure lime juice

ice

ginger beer

pineapple wedges and stem ginger, to decorate

method

1 Shake the first five ingredients vigorously over the ice until well frosted.

2 Strain the mixture into a tall chilled tumbler.

3 Top up with ginger beer and dress with the pineapple wedges and stem ginger.

ocean breeze

ingredients

SERVES 1

1 measure white rum

1 measure amaretto

$^1/_2$ measure blue curaçao

$^1/_2$ measure pineapple juice

ice

soda water

method

1 Shake the white rum, amaretto, blue curaçao and pineapple juice together over ice.

2 Pour into a tall glass and top up with soda water to taste.

plantation punch

ingredients

SERVES 1

2 measures dark rum

1 measure Southern Comfort

1 measure lemon juice

ice

1 tsp brown sugar

sparkling water

1 tsp ruby port

method

1 Shake the first three ingredients vigorously over the ice with the brown sugar until well frosted.

2 Strain into a tall, chilled glass and fill, almost to the rim, with sparkling water.

3 Float the port on top by pouring it gently over the back of a teaspoon.

peach daiquiri

ingredients

SERVES 1

2 measures white rum

1 measure lime juice

$1/2$ tsp sugar syrup

$1/2$ peach, peeled, stoned and chopped

method

1 Blend the ingredients together in a blender until smooth, then pour, without straining, into a chilled tumbler.

shanghai

ingredients

SERVES 1

4 measures dark rum

1 measure pastis

3 measures lemon juice

2 dashes grenadine

cracked ice

lemon slice and cocktail cherry, to decorate

method

1 Shake the first four ingredients together over the ice until well frosted.

2 Strain into a chilled glass and dress with the slice of lemon and the cherry.

hurricane

ingredients

SERVES 1

ice

4 measures dark rum

1 measure lemon juice

2 measures sweet fruit cocktail or juice (passion fruit and orange are the usual)

soda water

orange slice and cherries, to decorate

method

1 Fill a tall cocktail glass or highball glass with the ice. Shake the rum, lemon juice and sweet fruit cocktail until well combined and pour into the chilled glass.

2 Top up with soda water and dress with the orange slice and cherries.

rum cooler

ingredients

SERVES 1

2 ice cubes, plus extra to serve

juice of 1 lime

1^1/$_2$ measures rum

1^1/$_2$ measures pineapple juice

1 medium-ripe banana, cut into chunks

lime peel twist, to decorate

method

1 Blend the first five ingredients in a blender for about 1 minute or until smooth.

2 Pour over ice cubes into a chilled glass and finish with a twist of peel.

whiskey & brandy

Whiskey is not only the oldest known spirit, it also has a venerable pedigree in the cocktail bar, forming the basis of many famous, though uncomplicated, drinks. There are several different types of whiskey with distinctive flavours. Bourbon, distilled from a fermented cereal mash containing at least 51 per cent corn and aged for over six years, is the best-known American whiskey, so it is not surprising that it features in a number of classic cocktail recipes. Also American, as well as Canadian, rye whiskey is made from cereals containing at least 51 per cent rye, while Canadian whiskey is made from a mixture of cereals that vary according to brand. Scotch whisky may be single malt or blended – the former, made from dried, fermented and distilled barley is matured for over 10 years and is too fine and expensive for cocktails. Blended whisky, a mixture of grain spirits and malt whiskies, is used however. Irish whiskey is similar but the barley is dried in a different way.

Unlike other spirits, brandy is distilled from fermented grape juice or wine. Some of the most celebrated cocktails are brandy-based but they are not very numerous, perhaps because of its very distinctive flavour. Fruit brandies, such as Calvados, are also used in cocktails.

manhattan

ingredients

SERVES 1

dash Angostura bitters
3 measures rye whiskey
1 measure sweet vermouth
cracked ice
cocktail cherry, to decorate

method

1 Shake the first three ingredients together over the ice and mix well.

2 Strain into a chilled glass and decorate with the cherry.

mint julep

ingredients

SERVES 1

leaves from 1 fresh mint sprig, plus an extra sprig, to decorate

1 tbsp sugar syrup

crushed ice

3 measures bourbon

method

1 Put the mint leaves and sugar syrup into a small chilled glass and mash with a teaspoon. Add the ice and shake before adding the bourbon.

2 Dress with the mint sprig.

whisky sour

ingredients

SERVES 1

1 measure lemon or lime juice

2 measures blended whisky

1 tsp icing sugar or sugar syrup

ice

lime or lemon slice and cocktail cherry, to decorate

method

1 Shake the lemon juice, whisky and sugar well over the ice and strain into a cocktail glass.

2 Dress with the slice of lime and the cherry.

godfather

ingredients

SERVES 1

cracked ice

2 measures Scotch whisky

1 measure amaretto

method

1 Fill a chilled glass with the ice.

2 Pour in the whisky and amaretto and stir to mix.

thai cocktail sling

ingredients

SERVES 1

2 tbsp whiskey

1 tbsp cherry brandy

1 tbsp orange-flavoured liqueur

1 tbsp lime juice

1 tsp jaggery or coarse brown sugar

dash Angostura bitters

crushed ice

2 ice cubes

$1/2$ cup pineapple juice

1 small pineapple wedge, to decorate

method

1 Shake the first six ingredients well over the crushed ice until frosted. Place the ice cubes in a large glass.

2 Pour the cocktail over and top up with the pineapple juice.

3 Dress with the pineapple wedge.

brooklyn

ingredients

SERVES 1

1 measure rye whiskey

1/2 measure sweet vermouth

dash maraschino

dash Amer Picon or Angostura bitters

ice

cocktail cherry, to decorate

method

1 Shake the first four ingredients together over the ice to chill, then strain into a chilled cocktail glass.

2 Add the cherry to finish.

new yorker

ingredients

SERVES 1

2 measures Jack Daniels

1/2 measure fresh lime juice

1/2 measure grenadine

ice

orange peel twist, to decorate

method

1 Shake the first three ingredients together over the ice until frosted.

2 Pour into a chilled cocktail glass and serve with the orange peel twist.

commodore

ingredients

SERVES 1

4 measures rye whiskey

1 measure fresh lime juice

2 dashes orange bitters

sugar, to taste

ice

lime peel twist

method

1 Shake the first four ingredients together over the ice until well frosted.

2 Strain into a small tumbler or cocktail glass and dress with the twist of lime peel.

millionaire cocktail

ingredients

SERVES 1

$2/3$ measure bourbon

$1/3$ measure Cointreau

2 dashes grenadine

1 egg white

ice

method

1 Shake the first four ingredients over the ice.

2 Strain into a cocktail glass.

sparkling diamond

ingredients

SERVES 1

$1/4$ measure peppermint schnapps

$1/4$ measure white crème de cacao

$1/4$ measure Southern Comfort

$1/4$ measure lemon juice

crushed ice

method

1 Shake the first four ingredients over the ice.

2 Strain into a chilled shot glass and add a small spoonful of crushed ice.

strawberry kiss

ingredients

SERVES 1

1 measure Jack Daniels

1 measure strawberry syrup

3 strawberries

crushed ice

single cream

method

1 Blend the first four ingredients together in a blender.

2 Pour into a chilled glass and gently float the cream on top.

brandy cocktail

ingredients

SERVES 1

cracked ice

dash Angostura bitters

2 measures brandy

1/2 tsp sugar syrup

lemon slice, to decorate

method

1 Put the ice into a cocktail shaker with a dash of Angostura bitters, the brandy and the sugar syrup.

2 Shake vigorously until well frosted, then strain into a chilled cocktail glass and dress with the slice of lemon.

sweet singapore sling

ingredients

SERVES 1

1 measure gin

2 measures cherry brandy

dash lemon juice

cracked ice

soda water

cocktail cherry, to decorate

method

1 Shake the first three ingredients vigorously over the ice until well frosted.

2 Half fill a chilled tumbler with cracked ice and strain in the cocktail.

3 Top up with soda water and decorate with the cherry.

american rolls-royce

ingredients

SERVES 1

2 measures brandy

2 measures orange juice

1 measure triple sec

ice

method

1 Shake the first three ingredients together over the ice until well frosted.

2 Strain into a chilled glass.

stars & stripes

ingredients

SERVES 1

$^3/_4$ measure chilled cherry brandy

$^3/_4$ measure chilled blue curaçao

$1^1/_2$ measures chilled light cream

method

1 Pour the cherry brandy into a chilled shot glass.

2 With a steady hand, gently pour in the curaçao to make a second layer and, finally, gently pour in the cream.

country cousin collins

ingredients

SERVES 1

2 measures apple brandy

1 measure lemon juice

$1/2$ tsp sugar syrup

crushed ice

dash orange bitters

sparkling water

lemon slices, to decorate

method

1 Blend the first three ingredients with the ice in a blender and add a dash of orange bitters.

2 Pour into a chilled tumbler and top up with sparkling water.

3 Stir gently and dress with the slices of lemon.

cherry kitsch

ingredients

SERVES 1

1 measure cherry brandy

2 measures pineapple juice

$1/2$ measure kirsch

1 egg white

crushed ice

frozen cocktail cherry, to decorate

method

1 Shake the cherry brandy, pineapple juice, kirsch and egg white well over the ice until frosted.

2 Pour into a chilled tall thin glass and top with the cherry.

napoleon

ingredients

SERVES 1

1 measure Mandarine Napoléon
1 measure cherry brandy
ice
lemonade

method

1 Pour the liqueurs into a highball glass filled with the ice.

2 Stir gently and then gradually top up with the lemonade.

moonraker

ingredients

SERVES 1

cracked ice

dash Pernod

1 measure brandy

1 measure peach brandy

1 measure quinquina

method

1 Put the cracked ice into a mixing glass. Dash Pernod over the ice and pour in the brandy, peach brandy and quinquina.

2 Stir well to mix, then strain into a chilled glass.

black magic

ingredients

SERVES 1

1 1/4 measures cognac
1/2 measure chocolate liqueur
3/4 measure mandarin liqueur
ice
1 tbsp cream
chocolate flake, to decorate

method

1 Stir the first three ingredients over the ice in a mixing glass.

2 Strain into a chilled cocktail glass and carefully float the cream on top.

3 Dress with the chocolate flake.

all things bubbly

If cocktails turn any occasion into a party, those made with sparkling wine or, better still, champagne will transform it into a celebration. Champagne comes only from a delimited region of France and the name is protected. It is a sparkling wine produced as a result of secondary fermentation in the bottle, a special technique developed in the Champagne region. Vintage wines are too fine and costly for cocktails and even non-vintage champagne is expensive. However, combining it with other ingredients, such as fruit juice, in a cocktail does make it go further and provides an opportunity to give your guests a special treat. After all, there is little more elegant and delightful than a champagne breakfast. Sparkling wines, which may be made by a number of different methods, are a more economical substitute, especially if you are entertaining a large number of guests. There are some extremely drinkable bottles available.

Take care when opening champagne or other sparkling wines which have a wire cage fitted over the cork. Obviously, you should never shake the bottle unless you are a winning racing driver, but the force behind the cork is very considerable so make sure that you are not inadvertently pointing it towards someone's face. Also, do not let go of the cork once you have released the wire.

champagne cocktail

ingredients

SERVES 1

1 sugar cube
2 dashes Angostura bitters
1 measure brandy
chilled champagne

method

1 Place the sugar cube with the bitters in the bottom of a chilled flute.

2 Pour on the brandy and top up slowly with champagne.

buck's fizz

ingredients

SERVES 1

2 measures chilled fresh orange juice

2 measures chilled champagne

method

1 Half fill a chilled flute with orange juice, then gently pour in the chilled champagne.

kir royale

ingredients

SERVES 1

few drops cassis, or to taste
$1/2$ measure brandy
chilled champagne

method

1 Put the cassis and brandy into the bottom of a flute.

2 Fill up with champagne.

bellini

ingredients

SERVES 1

1 measure fresh peach juice, made from lightly sweetened, peeled and blended peaches

icing sugar

3 measures chilled champagne

method

1 Dip the rim of a champagne flute in some peach juice and then in some sugar to create a sugar-frosted effect. Set aside to dry.

2 Pour the rest of the peach juice into the chilled flute. Carefully top up with champagne.

mimosa

ingredients

SERVES 1

flesh of 1 passion fruit

$1/2$ measure orange curaçao

crushed ice

chilled champagne

star fruit slice, to decorate

method

1 Scoop out the passion fruit flesh into a jug or shaker and shake with the curaçao and a little ice until frosted.

2 Pour into the bottom of a champagne flute and top up with champagne.

3 Dress with the slice of star fruit.

chicago

ingredients

SERVES 1

egg white or lemon juice

icing sugar

1 measure brandy

1 dash Cointreau

1 dash Angostura bitters

ice

champagne

method

1 Frost the rim of a glass with the egg white and sugar.

2 Shake the next three ingredients together with the ice until frosted.

3 Strain into the prepared glass and top up with champagne.

black velvet

ingredients

SERVES 1

chilled Guinness
chilled champagne

method

1 Pour both drinks in equal quantities carefully into a long beer or highball glass.

serpentine

ingredients

SERVES 1

$^1/_2$ measure green crème de menthe

cracked ice

lime peel curl or twist

champagne, chilled

1 tsp lime zest, to decorate

method

1 Pour the crème de menthe into the bottom of a flute with the ice and the curl of lime peel.

2 Top up with champagne and dress with the sprinkle of lime zest.

royal julep

ingredients

SERVES 1

1 sugar lump

3 sprigs fresh mint, plus extra to decorate

1 measure Jack Daniels

chilled champagne

method

1 In a small glass, crush the sugar and mint together with a little of the whiskey. When the sugar has dissolved, strain it into a chilled flute with the rest of the whiskey, and top up with champagne.

2 Decorate with the mint sprigs.

long tall sally

ingredients

SERVES 1

$1/4$ measure brandy

$1/4$ measure dry vermouth

$1/4$ measure Galliano

$1/4$ measure mandarin liqueur

ice

champagne or sparkling wine

method

1 Stir the first four ingredients over ice and pour into a tall chilled glass.

2 Top up with champagne.

james bond

ingredients

SERVES 1

1 sugar cube

2 dashes Angostura bitters

1 measure chilled vodka

chilled champagne

method

1 Moisten the sugar cube with the bitters and place in the bottom of a chilled glass.

2 Cover with the vodka and then top up with champagne.

le crystal

ingredients

SERVES 1

$1/2$ measure Poire William

1 dash orange curaçao

ice

champagne

fresh pear slice, to decorate

method

1 Shake the first two ingredients over the ice until really cold.

2 Pour into a flute and top up with champagne.

3 Dress with the slice of pear.

midnight cocktail

ingredients

SERVES 1

1 measure raspberry vodka

1 measure fresh raspberry juice

1 measure orange juice

ice

chilled champagne

raspberries, to decorate

method

1 Shake the vodka, raspberry juice and orange juice vigorously over the ice until well frosted.

2 Strain into a chilled flute and top up with champagne.

3 Stir gently to mix and dress with some raspberries.

grape expectations

ingredients

SERVES 1

5–6 red or black grapes

ice

splash of mandarin liqueur

chilled pink champagne

method

1 Save 2 grapes for the glass. Crush the others in a small bowl. Add the ice and the liqueur, stir well, and strain into a chilled glass.

2 Fill up with champagne.

3 Halve the remaining grapes and add to the glass.

pick-me-up

ingredients

SERVES 1

ice

3 dashes Fernet Branca

3 dashes curaçao

1 measure brandy

champagne, chilled

lemon slice, to decorate

method

1 Place the ice in a wine glass to chill.

2 Stir in the next three ingredients gradually and top up with champagne.

3 Decorate with the lemon slice.

sparkling gold

ingredients

SERVES 1

1 measure golden rum

$1/2$ measure Cointreau

chilled champagne

method

1 Pour the rum and liqueur into a chilled glass and top up with champagne.

french 75

ingredients

SERVES 1

2 measures brandy

1 measure lemon juice

1 tbsp sugar syrup

cracked ice

chilled champagne

lemon peel twist, to decorate

method

1 Shake the first three ingredients vigorously over the ice until well frosted.

2 Strain into a chilled glass and top up with champagne.

3 Dress with the twist of lemon.

caribbean champagne

ingredients

SERVES 1

$1/2$ measure white rum
$1/2$ measure crème de banane
chilled champagne
banana slices, to decorate

method

1 Pour the rum and crème de banane into a chilled flute.

2 Top up with champagne.

3 Stir gently to mix and dress with the slices of banana.

velvet mule

ingredients

SERVES 1

1 measure cassis

1 measure black Sambuca

2 measures ginger wine

ice

cola

soda water or sparkling white wine

method

1 Stir the first three ingredients over the ice until well frosted.

2 Strain into a frosted flute and top up with equal quantities of cola and soda water.

disco dancer

ingredients

SERVES 1

1 measure crème de banane

1 measure rum

few drops Angostura bitters

ice

sparkling white wine

method

1 Shake the first three ingredients well over the ice.

2 Pour into a glass and top up with sparkling wine to taste.

flirtini

ingredients

SERVES 1

1/4 slice fresh pineapple, chopped

1/2 measure chilled Cointreau

1/2 measure chilled vodka

1 measure chilled pineapple juice

chilled champagne or sparkling white wine

method

1 Put the pineapple and Cointreau into a mixing glass or jug and stir with a spoon to crush the pineapple.

2 Add the vodka and pineapple juice and stir well, then strain into a glass.

3 Top up with champagne.

pink sherbet royale

ingredients

SERVES 2

1½ cups sparkling white wine, really cold

2 measures cassis

1 measure brandy

crushed ice

blackberries, to decorate

method

1 Blend half the wine in a blender with the cassis, brandy and ice until really cold and frosted.

2 Slowly whisk in a little more wine and pour into tall thin glasses.

3 Dress with the blackberries.

raspberry lemonade

ingredients

SERVES 4

2 lemons

115 g/4 oz icing sugar

115 g/4 oz fresh raspberries

few drops vanilla extract

crushed ice

ice cubes

iced sparkling water

lemon balm sprigs, to decorate

method

1 Cut the ends off the lemons, scoop out and chop the flesh and place in a blender with the sugar, raspberries, vanilla extract and ice. Blend until smooth.

2 Strain into tall glasses and top up with ice cubes and sparkling water.

3 Dress with sprigs of lemon balm.

apple fizz

ingredients

SERVES 1

125 ml/4 fl oz sparkling cider or apple juice

1 measure Calvados

juice of $1/2$ lemon

1 tbsp egg white

generous pinch sugar

ice

method

1 Shake the first five ingredients together over the ice and pour immediately into a glass.

non-alcoholic

There are many reasons why some of your guests may not want to consume alcoholic drinks, particularly ones that can be as potent as some cocktails. They may be under age, driving, pregnant, on medication, slimming, focusing on a healthy lifestyle, concerned about over-indulgence in alcohol or simply not like it. However, cocktails are fun and it seems very unfair if those who don't drink alcohol are unable to join in. Sometimes called 'mocktails', these innocuous drinks are the answer – colourful concoctions with adult flavours that are mostly made in the same ways as their alcoholic cousins.

In fact, many of these recipes are 'innocent' versions of well-known and classic cocktails but they are more subtle than the simple omission of the alcoholic ingredients. Just leaving out the spirit base would make the drink thin and lifeless, while omitting alcoholic mixers would spoil the flavour. Clever substitutes and appropriate alternatives have been used to give these drinks the zing that is characteristic of cocktails.

Equally, some of these non-alcoholic adult drinks have been specially created without any reference to the traditional cocktail bar. Delicious combinations of fruit juices, vegetable juices, fresh berries and sparkling mixers give them a unique flavour that is all their own.

shirley temple

ingredients

SERVES 1

2 measures lemon juice

$^1/_2$ measure grenadine

$^1/_2$ measure sugar syrup

cracked ice

ginger ale

orange slice and cocktail cherry, to decorate

method

1 Shake the lemon juice, grenadine and sugar syrup vigorously over the ice until well frosted.

2 Strain into a small, chilled glass half filled with cracked ice. Top up with ginger ale.

3 Dress with the orange slice and the cocktail cherry.

virgin mary

ingredients

SERVES 1

3 measures tomato juice

1 measure lemon juice

2 dashes Worcestershire sauce

1 dash Tabasco sauce

cracked ice

pinch celery salt

pepper

lemon slice and celery stick, to decorate

method

1 Shake the first four ingredients vigorously over the ice and season with celery salt and pepper. Strain into a chilled glass.

2 Dress with the lemon slice and the celery stick.

soft sangria

ingredients

SERVES 4

1.2 litres/2 pints red grape juice

225 ml/8 fl oz orange juice

3 measures cranberry juice

2 measures lemon juice

2 measures lime juice

4 measures sugar syrup

ice

lemon and lime slices

method

1 Pour all the juices and the sugar syrup into a chilled punch bowl and stir well.

2 Add the ice and the lemon and lime slices and serve in chilled glasses.

faux kir royale

ingredients

SERVES 1

cracked ice

$1^1/_2$ measures raspberry syrup

sparkling apple juice

method

1 Put the ice into a mixing glass.

2 Pour the raspberry syrup over the ice. Stir well to mix, then strain into a wine glass.

3 Top up with apple juice and stir.

baby bellini

ingredients

SERVES 6

2 measures peach juice

1 measure lemon juice

sparkling apple juice

method

1 Pour the peach juice and lemon juice into a chilled champagne flute and stir well.

2 Top up with the apple juice and stir.

cool collins

ingredients

SERVES 6

6 fresh mint leaves

1 tsp icing sugar

2 measures lemon juice

cracked ice

sparkling water

fresh mint sprigs and lemon slices, to decorate

method

1 Put the mint leaves into a tall chilled tumbler and add the sugar and lemon juice. Crush the leaves with a spoon until the sugar has dissolved.

2 Fill the glass with cracked ice and top up with sparkling water.

3 Stir gently and dress with the fresh mint sprigs and the lemon slices.

mini colada

ingredients

SERVES 2

6 measures cold milk

4 measures pineapple nectar

3 measures coconut cream

crushed ice

pineapple cubes and cocktail cherries, to decorate

method

1 Shake the first four ingredients over the ice until well chilled.

2 Pour into long glasses, add more ice and dress with the pieces of pineapple and the cherries.

cranberry punch

ingredients

SERVES 10

600 ml/1 pint cranberry juice

600 ml/1 pint orange juice

150 ml/5 fl oz water

$1/2$ tsp ground ginger

$1/4$ tsp cinnamon

$1/4$ tsp freshly grated nutmeg

cracked ice, if serving cold

frozen cranberries and their leaves, to decorate

method

1 Put the first six ingredients into a saucepan and bring to the boil. Reduce the heat and simmer for 5 minutes.

2 Remove from the heat and pour into heatproof glasses.

3 Chill and add cracked ice if serving cold. Decorate with the cranberries and their leaves.

strawberry colada

ingredients

SERVES 2

450 g/1 lb strawberries

125 ml/4 fl oz coconut cream

600 ml/1 pint chilled pineapple juice

method

1 Reserve four strawberries to decorate. Halve the remainder and place in the blender.

2 Add the coconut cream and pineapple juice and blend until smooth, then pour into chilled glasses and dress with the reserved strawberries.

pear & raspberry delight

ingredients

SERVES 2

2 large ripe Anjou pears, peeled, cored and chopped

140 g/5 oz frozen raspberries

175 ml/6 fl oz ice-cold water

honey, to taste

raspberries, to decorate

method

1 Put the pears into a blender with the raspberries and water and blend until smooth.

2 Taste and sweeten with honey if the raspberries are a little sharp.

3 Pour into glasses and dress with the raspberries.

perky pineapple

ingredients

SERVES 4

cracked ice

2 bananas

225 ml/8 fl oz pineapple juice, chilled

125 ml/4 fl oz lime juice

pineapple slices, to decorate

method

1 Put the cracked ice into a blender. Peel the bananas and slice directly into the blender. Add the pineapple and lime juice and blend until smooth.

2 Pour into chilled glasses and dress with the slices of pineapple.

ginger fizz

ingredients

SERVES 1

ginger ale

fresh mint sprigs

cracked ice

raspberries and a sprig of mint, to decorate

method

1 Put the ginger ale and several mint leaves into a blender and blend together.

2 Strain into a chilled highball glass filled two-thirds with the ice. Dress with the raspberries and the mint sprig.

long boat

ingredients

SERVES 1

ice

1 measure lime cordial

ginger beer

lime wedge and mint sprig, to decorate

method

1 Fill a chilled highball or tall glass two-thirds full with the ice and pour in the lime cordial.

2 Top up with ginger beer and stir gently.

3 Decorate with the lime wedge and the mint sprig.

st. clements

ingredients

SERVES 2

ice cubes

2 measures orange juice

2 measures bitter lemon

orange and lemon slices, to decorate

method

1 Put the ice cubes into a chilled tumbler. Pour in the orange juice and bitter lemon.

2 Stir gently and dress with the slices of orange and lemon.

salty puppy

ingredients

SERVES 6

sugar

coarse salt

lime wedge

cracked ice

$1/2$ measure lime juice

grapefruit juice

method

1 Mix equal quantities of sugar and salt in a saucer. Rub the rim of a small, chilled tumbler with the lime and dip in the sugar and salt mixture to frost.

2 Fill the glass with the ice and pour the lime juice over.

3 Top up with the grapefruit juice.

coconut islander

ingredients

SERVES 1

1 pineapple

4 measures pineapple juice

4 tbsp creamed coconut

4 measures milk

2 tbsp crushed pineapple

3 tbsp shredded coconut

crushed ice

cherry, to decorate

method

1 Cut the top off the pineapple and remove the flesh.

2 Blend all the ingredients except the cherry in a blender with a little ice.

3 Serve in the pineapple and decorate with the cherry.

cranberry energizer

ingredients

SERVES 2

300 ml/10 fl oz cranberry juice
125 ml/4 fl oz orange juice
55 g/2 oz fresh raspberries
1 tbsp lemon juice
fresh orange slices, to decorate

method

1 Pour the cranberry juice and orange juice into a blender and blend gently until combined.

2 Add the raspberries and lemon juice and blend until smooth.

3 Pour the mixture into glasses and dress with the slices of orange.

citrus fizz

ingredients

SERVES 1

2 measures fresh orange juice, chilled

icing sugar

squeeze lime juice

few drops Angostura bitters

2–3 measures sparkling water, chilled

method

1 Rub the rim of a flute with orange or lime juice and dip into icing sugar.

2 Stir the rest of the juices together with the bitters and then pour into the glass.

3 Add sparkling water to taste.

cocobelle

ingredients

SERVES 1

3 measures cold milk

1 measure coconut cream

2 scoops vanilla ice cream

3–4 ice cubes

dash grenadine

desiccated coconut, toasted, to decorate

method

1 Blend the first four ingredients in a blender until slushy.

2 Chill a tall glass and gently dribble a few splashes of grenadine down the insides.

3 Pour in the slush slowly and top with the toasted coconut.

italian soda

ingredients

SERVES 1

cracked ice

1^1/$_2$ measures hazelnut syrup

sparkling water

lime slice, to decorate

method

1 Fill a chilled glass with the ice.

2 Pour the hazelnut syrup over and top up with sparkling water.

3 Stir gently and dress with the slice of lime.

cherry orchard

ingredients

SERVES 1

1 measure apple juice

1 measure pear juice

2 measures cranberry juice

ice

pink lemonade or cherryade

cocktail cherry and a pineapple wedge, to decorate

method

1 Mix the fruit juices together over the ice in a chilled glass.

2 Top up with lemonade to taste and dress with the cherry and pineapple.

cocoberry

ingredients

SERVES 1

85 g/3 oz raspberries

crushed ice

1 measure coconut cream

150 ml/5 fl oz pineapple juice

pineapple wedge and fresh raspberries, to decorate

method

1 Press the raspberries through a strainer with the back of a spoon and transfer the purée to a blender.

2 Add the ice, coconut cream and the pineapple juice. Blend until smooth, then pour the mixture, without straining, into a chilled tumbler.

3 Dress with the pineapple wedge and fresh raspberries.

grapefruit cooler

ingredients

SERVES 6

55 g/2 oz fresh mint
2 measures sugar syrup
450 ml/16 fl oz grapefruit juice
4 measures lemon juice
cracked ice
sparkling mineral water
fresh mint sprigs, to decorate

method

1 Crush the fresh mint leaves in a small bowl with the sugar syrup. Set aside for at least 2 hours to steep, mashing again from time to time.

2 Strain into a jug and add the grapefruit juice and lemon juice. Cover with clingfilm and chill for at least 2 hours, until required.

3 To serve, fill 6 chilled glasses with the ice. Divide the cocktail between the glasses and top up with sparkling water.

4 Dress with the mint sprigs.

lemon fizz

ingredients

SERVES 1

2 fresh lemons

crushed ice

peel of $1/2$ lemon

1 tbsp sugar

iced lemonade

method

1 Squeeze the lemons and pour the juice into a chilled highball glass filled with the ice.

2 Add the piece of peel and sugar to taste and stir briefly.

3 Top up with lemonade to taste.